I Love You Day and Night

by Alexandra Vasiliu

illustrations by Mel Darmawan

Stairway Books
2025

You are my flower and my greatest joy.

Your smile lights up my world.

Your joy is my joy.

You are my dream come true.

You count your blessings one by one,

but know that
you are my greatest blessing.

I love you every winter.

You are
my sweet little angel.

but know that
you are the beautiful star
of my heart.

My dear child,
you are the light of my life,

I love you
day and night,
every season,
all year long.

For my precious son —
you are my heart. – A.V.

For all the beautiful children reading this book —
I hope you know you are well-loved. – A.V.

If you enjoy this book, please recommend it to your friends and write a brief Amazon review. Your support helps me more than you can imagine and allows me to continue writing more inspiring picture books.
Thank you so much. – A.V.

Text and illustrations copyright © 2025 by Alexandra Vasiliu
Visit the author's website at www.alexandravasiliu.net

All rights reserved. Printed in the United States of America. Published by Stairway Books. No part of this publication may be reproduced, scanned, downloaded, decompiled, reverse-engineered, stored in any retrieval system, or transmitted in any form by any means, including photocopying, recording, or other electronic or mechanical methods, or otherwise, without the prior written permission of the author or publisher. Piracy of copyrighted materials is a criminal offense. Purchase only authorized editions. The publisher has no control over and does not assume any responsibility for third-party websites or their content.

For permission requests, please contact Alexandra Vasiliu at Stairway Books, 3324 E Ray Rd #1228, Higley, AZ 85236, or at alexandra@alexandravasiliu.net.

I Love You Day and Night by Alexandra Vasiliu and illustrated by Mel Darmawan. Stairway Books, 2025

ISBN-13: 978-1-963003-91-8

First US paperback edition, June 2025

Editing services provided by Melanie Underwood at www.melanieunderwood.co.uk

Illustrations by Mel Darmawan

www.ingramcontent.com/pod-product-compliance
Lightning Source LLC
Chambersburg PA
CBHW040031050426
42453CB00002B/82